Losing the
Horizon

Losing the Horizon

Poems

Priscilla Orr

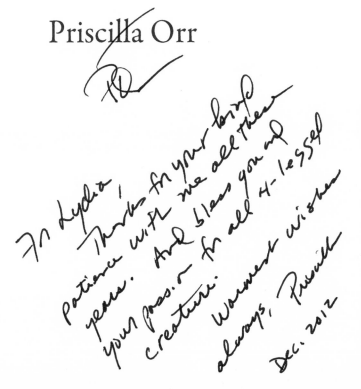

To Lydia,
Thanks for your love &
patience with me all these
years. And bless you and
your passion for all 4-legged
creatures.
Warmest wishes
always, Russell
Dec. 2012

Cover design by Pam & Harry Bernard
Interior layout by Scribe Freelance | www.scribefreelance.com
Cover photo and painting by Pam Bernard
Author photo by Harry Bernard

Published by:
Hannacroix Creek Books, Inc.
1127 High Ridge Road, #110
Stamford, Connecticut 06905 USA
http://www.hannacroixcreekbooks.com | e-mail: hannacroix@aol.com
Follow us on twitter: www.twitter.com/hannacroixcreek

ISBN: 978-1-889262-35-2 (trade paperback)
1-889262-35-8

Library of Congress Cataloging-in-Publication Data

Orr, Priscilla.
Losing the horizon : poems / Priscilla Orr. p. cm.
ISBN 978-1-889262-35-2 (alk. paper) I.
Title.
PS3615.R5887L67 2013
811'.6--dc23

2012020906

For now had come that moment, that hesitation,
when dawn trembles and night pauses...

From *To the Lighthouse*
—Virginia Woolf

For the friends who have been my family all these years;
you know who you are.

Especially in memory of Lynne, for
***Kristi, Linda, Sandy & Joe** and*
*always for **Margaret***

Contents

I

The Bright Blooming

The Ether

While hiking near the tree line, my spaniel
nudges the half-rotted carcass of a small bird.
Stepping through layered leaf piles
I call her away, but she hesitates,
enchanted by the little cadaver.

Startled by the whoosh whoosh woo
of the wind through maple and oak limb,
she sprints after me, ears flailing.

Wind, wave, light—
who can discern one stirring from another?
Souls shunted through—
how many hover here?

Even the promise of summer sun
seems lost while my own dear dead
flit and dart about. Are you
among them, my friend?
Or do I hear simply the whistling
whorl from that other world.

Western Union,
Great Falls, Montana, 1968

My mom was the night manager.
It paid more. I was in Missoula,
in college. Hugo and the other writers
drank in Eddie's bar. But I was lost
in that crowd. So I drank at the Ox,
where rumor had it when they yelled
"stretch one," Gus flattened a beef mound
under his armpit before slapping it on the grill.
I watched but never saw him do it.

Meanwhile, my mother, in Great Falls,
got robbed at gunpoint. The robber
locked her in the back closet,
where she heard the teletype ticking,
news pouring in from the East.
A patrolman noted the late brightly lit office,
found her, offered her a ride home,
but she had wet herself, that gun barrel
so close to her heart. Ashamed,
she went home alone in a taxi.

So much I've forgotten— a bourbon
on the rocks when the boss snapped
at her, or when the child support
never came; the slight flush when the nuns
told her *no communion* for a divorced woman.
She would swallow it all in her drink.

That gunman came back a year later.
But this time she went to the closet
as if it were a drill. I can almost hear
the rhythmic click of her high heels on tile.
Outside a truck spewed up grit and salt
on plowed walks and parked cars
while a Chinook came down from Choteau—
its dry wind melting the mound of muddied snow.

Once My Husband

He arrives at the poetry reading
lilies ablaze on one arm, a cane on the other.
Haltingly he walks into a maze
of books, calendars, and a café.
His face scans the aisles for me.
Married again with three children,
his MS progressing, he's not the cocky
young man. He sits a bit off
from the others, face averted
as I read. I'm nervous.

Back then, the poems scared us.
Whenever I wrote, he'd come up behind me
offering juice or lunch, anything
to peer over my shoulder, to find
whatever wildness in me was on the page.
Even now, I wonder what might hurt him,

what I should hide. But later, when we have coffee,
he strokes the book cover, his hand gliding
over my name. He's shy, but he's clearly pleased,
remembering fragments, people we knew,
places we lived.

Awed by what falls away,
from what terrible mistakes we make—
I nearly burn my tongue.

When the Body Takes Over

The day my dog died, the vet put us in a room
with a door open to the outside. We sat on the floor,
her little black nose sniffing air for any scent.
I wrapped my down vest around her, and she,
who never liked restraint, let me hold her,
relaxed into my arms, her freckled snout
reaching up to lick my nose.

My vet explained how the anesthetic
works. Sometimes an animal dies
before the fluid is emptied from the large syringe.
In shock, I never realized that once they took
her from my arms I would not hold her again.
There was no romance in this death, just a kind
of automatic pilot, the body taking over for me.
As I murmured to her, stroked her forehead
her eyes began to glaze over.
"Are you leaving me, darling?" I asked.

I can't seem to get over it—how we remember the image
but forget the depth of any wrenching pain,
brown drops of blood on the sheet with
my mother's body,
the emergence of the skeleton just beneath the skin
in my friend with cancer. When it returns, that pain,
it smacks the body so hard, so fast, there is no escape.
We may need to numb our way towards death,
but once it comes, we are sucker-punched,
TKO'd, blitzed with anguish. That we survive
is a miracle of the body as much as the soul——
or maybe a miracle the body makes for the soul.

15

Skating

In memory of Lynne S. Dumas

Even with a trainer,
Lynne clung to the side rail
one hand cupped, ready to grip
as he coaxed her onto the rink.

Over forty, this was no gold medal
dream. Just the uncut nerve of her leg
thrust forward in a wobble and bob
seemed Olympic enough.

To lift off, she must trust the sharp-edged
steel to cut into the grain of the ice,
let loose her clutched hand and glide.

I never saw her skate, never saw the downy
lake surface on which she flew.
Missed her first glide, the backward drift,
the gentle arc of her ¾ spin.

In our infinite motion,
how heroic the human heart,
always a salchow and a triple lutz
ahead of our lumbering selves.

Grading Papers at 10 PM

I'm too old for this, I'm thinking as I wade
through the pile of narratives,
my eye lifting up to the mute television for some relief.
It's only the second week of the semester, and already I'm weary,

when I read: *I'd never been to a funeral.*
I didn't want to look at his body, but my dad
told me I had to man- up. Close your eyes,
my mom said, as if you are praying. That'll help.
Finally some energy in a piece I've read thousands of times,
but then he doesn't know what to do, disintegrates into cliché,

Now I know that every minute counts,
that you can't take people for granite.
I cross out *granite* and handwrite *granted* over it,
encourage him where I can. Feeling culpable,
I wonder how long I can do this,
stay fresh for each one of them.

When I return the paper, he looks for the grade first,
then reads my comments over and over
before slipping it into his book bag.

Losing the Horizon

after JFK Jr.

These weren't wax wings
soaring with the bravado of youth.
Nor was the sun a culprit,
unless its slow dip into that other
ocean can be blamed.

And the prince who was not a prince
grappled with the controls, two women
happily chattering near him. "I'm no
Lindbergh," he'd said to a friend.

Could they detect
his hunched shoulders stiffen as he raked
over the coastline, its small lights
little comfort as he made that last turn?

Did his heart thump and pound
in that final plunge, or did vertigo
protect them all to the point of impact.

What in us hungers to go back —
to mythic wings, a young man
charting the night sky?
What in us cannot reduce his yearning
to a failure to decode the instrument
panel — its minute flutter and flail.

Membrane

Tonight, during an asana—
pelvis breeched to the floor—
it comes in feathered light
waves, water and breath,
I nearly glide through.

But the scent of him, his
wild-eyed plunge into me
obliterates that other world.

Body, how easily I could abandon you.
How I need him to keep you close to me.

II

Night Pauses

A Late Flurry

for Madeline

Only our bodies age, I want to tell the young.
The heart pumps on while the rest of the body
wavers. Flesh puffs-up; hair thins.
We do what we can with the skin and the hair,
that which the young revere.

After all these years, my true voice
comes forward. Steadier now, it can
sing in nearly any key if my breath
begins low enough in the diaphragm,
gathers there before the ascent.

Or do I make this up, like I make my life?
Outside, another blizzard. I've dug a trench
where the dog can pee; her back legs tangle easily
in deeper snow. She sleeps by my chair as I type this.
In our slight reverie, a stint of light pierces the late flurry.

Forsaken

Robert trembled as he made his vows.
Carley wore a frilly dress—pink, black, and red ruffles.
My mother did not come.

I should have known
I already had given myself away—
the deep rose nail polish when I wanted white,
my hair cut too short, or the way I lost my breath
just before the ceremony. Then—I do, I do.
Now, I can risk anything but that.

~

In her last days, my mother rarely left her mobile home.
She'd go to McDonald's for coffee, the mall to walk,
the beauty school for a haircut,
Denny's for bacon and eggs.

~

My 83 year-old friend mows her own lawn,
plants impatiens. She wants to stay in her house,
but her adult kids want her someplace smaller,
safer. Should she move? Is she eating up their inheritance?

~

My old spaniel naps, her breath a cacophony
of rasp and sputter. One night, I went to the kitchen for a snack,
the blue TV light flickering. I turned to toss her
a chunk of manchego, but for the first time, she hadn't followed.
Startled by that vacant space, I went to wake her up.

~

All winter, storm winds bluster through.
Snow gathers layer upon layer. I can't seem to shake
the chill. Tonight four more inches of sleet land on the pile
It's the accretion, I say, to no-one in particular.
We collapse from the sheer weight of it all.

24

Late Bloomer

Oddly out of step, the one duckling scrambles
to catch the others, as the mother moves
forward. At the edge of their pond,

a few bread crumbs, an insistent hunger.
Like melody, a riff, a few notes,
I remember you in sweatpants
your bulk and sag loose beneath
cotton and a sweet blast of autumn sun
deceptive through tumbling leaves.

The duckling paddles just behind the others,
tiny webbed feet in furious motion,
Already, I am too fond of it.

Kaleidoscope

When March shepherds in the equinox,
that old angst returns—grief, a habit of mind—
pruning forsythia, staking peonies.
Rye seed scatters like wedding rice
from my hand while the dog wends through
muck and bramble flagging any scent.

Last spring, Lynne's birthday loomed.
Striking in a crisp black sheath,
cheeks plush, she raised her glass to us.
How could we not toast her life? At home,
buds erupted on the bare-limbed cherry.

By December, her skin receded; her skull
emerged. Another death to score in the pith
and pons of my brain. The dog unearths
a bone – gold tones weathered into fine lines.
I hold it up to my eye, kaleidoscope
of cartilage, brittle trail blocking my view.

The Mourner

for Paul

Casket already lowered into the ground,
clumps of earth sprayed over calla lilies,
he teeters there, while others make for car doors.
The thump and clunk of shovels echo after them.

Now atoms, traveling filaments of light, the dead
struggle to return to him. But severed from bone
or corpuscle, they are too light to perforate his grief.

In time, they learn to pierce through REM sleep—
loosen his eyelashes at first light—
as if they could dream him back into the world.

Poker Game

for Jimmy

In an old house off the Hudson River
Jimmy poaches pears, to top off
roast duck, potato soup, bourbon
or wine. With the wood stove crackle,
and Ella's crooning, we feast.
I love this house, brick alcove
stove in the kitchen, bluestone counters,
how the river barges flicker.

"Ante up," Paul deals. "I'm in"
yells Jimmy from the kitchen.
Wearing my lucky hat, I raise the pot.
Joe steals pennies from Sandy's pile.
But Sandy has a tell; her tongue curls
over her upper lip. I know I should fold.

Metronome

for Anita

Once, before her friend Sue died, she rented
a wheelchair fit for the dunes. Lean threads
of beach grass atop a sandbank rendered the shore
invisible from the street. But they heard
the smack and roar of waves on the tide flat,
then the slithering back of the undertow,
a kind of metronome calling them.

So she pushed that chair up the dune
trying not to breathe hard, not to distress
Sue who held her straw hat as they hit the crest,
wind rushing into them, white foam
dancing below. They paused before the descent,
wide chair wheels held by a brake.

At dusk, books unopened,
they murmured into the salt spray,
those iridescent moments of late day.

Sue gone now a year, she clamors
over the dune, shelters herself from the grit
and sting of sand in wind. With the sea in front,
sun behind, her dead serenade her, their reverie
muted by the whip and slap of wave upon wave.

Death Rites

My mother died in winter, hours before
the equinox. A priest smeared
little oil crosses over eyes, mouth, nostrils,
sealed her soul into her body. I didn't know

about the soul, how shamans prod it up the spine;
release it, or how Hindis anoint the body,
then purge it in fire. No long lament
or a soul might cling to the earth.

But my mother who hung onto her scapula,
little bone fragment of some saint,
wanted that priest. Last night I dreamt

I was buried face down, no coffin,
only earth – the fertile feel of it a kind
of cushion. Oddly unafraid, I waited to lift off,
whatever of me that was me, while my body fell

away. Was this what they felt as they lingered –
my friend, my mom – the body slightly tethered
to those they love; the spirit combustible:
indiscernible fuel of wind, water, and cloud.

Winter With Ice

In memory of my mother

When her dog died, she found herself oddly free.
So long had care-giving held her captive—
rushing home to let the dog out,
cooking ground chicken and rice to disguise the meds.

It had been a winter full of ice, no soft snow for them to walk
only salted sidewalks that ate at the pads of the dog's feet.
Grief already a resident, she did not try to fill the space
though a friend made her have the rug cleaned
to obliterate the remnants of those last months.

Too soon she found herself in the lush stark horror of April
daffodil and crocus—color everywhere.
Her mother had died in March so this was familiar—
the earth in thaw, and she still frozen.

How easily she was distracted,
her car drifting into the wrong lane,
a piece of food going down the wrong pipe.
Even though death startled her,
it was becoming clear how one
might slip out of life—
before the equinox,
before the bright blooming.

And When I'm Dead

for Margaret

Whatever you inherit, don't let it burden you.
Don't hold my favorite cup in your hand and weep.
Throw away the photos I cherished,
only smiling strangers to you.
Rip my diplomas from their gilded frames.
Put your own art in them.

Don't worry that my poems will disappear,
that no-one else will read them. I'm done.
Those who let my words fall over them have
taken what they needed. Don't
worry that I had no family. You
were the one who kept me here.

Who knows where my soul will hover.
Could be anywhere—split atoms in the ether
or, like a bundle of neutrinos,
it might slip through matter
as if it had never existed.

For awhile, your body will move toward the phone,
to call me while making cupcakes for the kids,
or to tell me of some small cruelty from work.
But sooner than I'd like to think it will just be memory
that resonates inside you as you hike Umstead,
or drive home from school. In these odd moments
you will talk with me as if I'm there.
If only I could hear you, as I hear you now.

III

St. Joseph's Academy
1955–1961

The Cuban Girls

we called them. Carmen spoke no English.
Sad-el-shoose, Sr. Leonard said, pointing to her oxfords.
Sad-el-shoose, Carmen would repeat, amiably.

They stuck together, their tongue an impenetrable code.
"No Spanish," Sr. Leonard said stamping her foot,
but she couldn't stop the lovely vowels spilling
from their mouths. Each night we *let* them play
their music ten or fifteen minutes before
clamoring for the Everly Brothers.

"I want you to tell me why you walked out on me.
I'm so lonesome everyday..." Girl-to-girl, we danced a swing,
our pleated skirts a halting swirl over bare knees.

One morning, we woke to shrieks and sobs,
the Cuban girls huddled together. Nuns cloaked
them, keeping us away. Bay of Pigs, we would learn.
We didn't get it then— the blockade, the politics; only
the grief seemed familiar—that inalienable ache for home.

Sunday at Dusk

The '56 Plymouth Fury
paused at the edge of the white stone
driveway. A two-toned blue, it blended
into twilight. I couldn't tell it was gone
until the little red lights blinked
before turning onto the road.
At least my mom did not see me fall.

Why cry now? A ninth grader might see.
Little stone imprint on my kneecaps
would bring a scowl from Sister Marie,
so I brush it, and head inside. By now
mom will be over the bay bridge.

As we line-up for supper Jo Mary asks
if I did the math homework.
She is eight, like me.
We're the youngest here.
The steam table looks bleak; white rice glints
under harsh light. As I hold out my plate,
red beans run into the cornbread.
Sr. Jean sees my frown, adds two chicken legs
instead of one to my plate. There is chocolate
pudding with whipped cream for dessert.

Why I Love Birthday Cake

My first year there, on my ninth birthday,
I told everyone it would be there,
but no-one had told my mom
to call the local bakery. So I came downstairs
having bragged to the other boarders.

The nuns had told my mom
about the monthly cake,
the one that they did for everyone
who had a birthday that month.

So it was the next year when it arrived
a white cake, icing glistening,
and pink loops around the edges,
requisite pink roses clustered in threes
Happy Birthday, Priscilla.

Set on the sideboard for my own disposal,
our only little freedom,
the birthday cake dried against the lace
doily. Even on the third day when the frosting
hardened, we still set upon the icing crust,
love, liquid on our tongues.

Canteen

At three pm, before study hall,
the green plywood lifted to open the canteen.
One treat allowed. Money helped. If you had it,
you could buy anything you wanted—a Dreamsicle
a Gold Brick chocolate bar. Why bother
with penny candy, the Mary Janes,
or turn-your-tongue-purple jaw breakers?

With a sugar high, we would fly
through the back playground,
peddle the merry-go-round,
until the peel of angelus bells.
Rickety-creak slowing spin,
we dragged our feet
till all riders emptied off.

Archie Comics

After supper, Sr. Leonard would ring
her little brass bell. She held a fist of letters
in her left hand. One by one, we sat alert

waiting for pink or cream envelopes.
My mother sent notes in green ink,
she thought black ink angry.
Her packages filled with pecan turtles
and Archie comics were a hit with my friends.

In a room where virgin girls in scuffed
shoes and pleated skirts waited
to hear the call of their name, I clung
to those squares of colored characters.
Veronica's dark hair fell to the side like mine.

May Day

In dress-white blouses and pleated skirts,
our saddle shoes polished to a shine,
we'd process in twos to the Virgin.

Moss hung from the pecan trees,
their shadow of a canopy
flung down the dirt foot path.

In the grotto, the Virgin waited.
Fresh white candles
burned beneath her.

Always, a diminutive blonde child
carried the crown of flowers
pink ribbons streaming.

Even though I'd sneak back here
in winter, see her chipped blue robe
and cracked face, I hungered

to hold the crown, to place
it over her bowed head —
lopsided flowers and all.

Payback

She was the tough nun, her fat little fist furiously ringing that bell.
Stand in line; stand up straight; sit down; get up, kneel at your bed;
lights out; don't squirm; be still. My last day was coming. I
promised everyone, I'd take the brass nugget out of her bell.
We imagined her frantic, shaking it, no sounds coming out.
I even mimicked her puffed out cheeks, my friends' laughter,
hysterical. *Do it*, they said. *She can't hurt you.*

We learn in ways we never expect. Even now, I see her, a short
round woman in black habit. Her white bib in contrast to her red
face as the bell makes no sound. She shudders ever so slightly, or
is it the quake of my own body from the din of the room,
all of them howling at my little trick,
the small ball bud from her bell buried in my bag.

Arrogance

There are times not to look back,
not to see your mother's face as you board
the bus for the convent school
or inhale diesel fuel from the Trailways
headed for New Orleans; not the time
to scream *take me home* as the driver
slams the luggage chamber, your suitcase
stored in the back well.

There are times not to go back
her niche in a Tucson cemetery, nor time to figure
how the mass of her body — soft tissue and bone —
can amount to one small white cardboard box.
Your last dog had more mass as you scattered
fragments of bone and ash along the shoreline.

Instead, have a favorite summer supper,
mozzarella, tomatoes, basil and olive oil.
She came from the world of Cheez Whiz,
highballs in tall glasses. Sometimes you think
you are better with your filtered water
and bolognaise, compared to her Chef Boyardee.

There are times not to regret how you thought
you could marry into Oyster Bay or Huntington Park,
and forget the house in Biloxi, a screened porch
with cement steps where you stood while Mother
put a bowl on your head to trim your bangs.
You squirmed even then, the hairline never straight.

Today your own little condo needs work.
Like your mother in her Tucson mobile home,
you can make your peace with it,
if you don't look back, if you don't look ahead.

From the Water Fountain, Biloxi, Mississippi, 1953

In the old five-and-dime, layers of shirts
and pants laid piled on tables for women
to sift through. One held up a plaid
short-sleeved shirt to a phantom
body – husband, son or lover. The dark blades
of those ceiling fans whirred that white noise
against the late afternoon heat.

Bored and thirsty, I found two erect towers
of cool water. On tiptoe, I wrestled my body up
until an arc of water splashed my face. So pleased
at my reach, I didn't even feel the yank
and tug of my body until I stumbled backwards.
What had I done? How had I misbehaved?

Then I saw the word Colored over one tower,
the word White over the other. I felt the stares,
the taut hold of my mother's arm, the strain in her face,
until the "but, Mom…" which escaped
my mouth was hushed in the summer hum.

Rosary on a Door

Left on the old door knob, the black beads and crucifix
hang haplessly, as if some soul could not quite abandon his faith.
Maybe a former altar boy left it here. As a kid,
he would have swung the censer, while kneeling
at the feet of his priest. White smoke swirled up, then
dissipated on the altar. Imagine the sock slipped down his foot,
but he can't turn to pull it up or he'll annoy the priest.
He can't stop an itch near his groin,
can't stop his mind's meanderings.

But the priest senses his wavering,
stares him down, and the itch goes away.
Ritual keeps him in line.
His is the faith of the young,
ones who believe everything
until their world fissures in some small way.

   Like this door,
pine crackled from wind and rain,
the frame never completely closes.

IV

Dawn Trembles

The Dover Effect

In its aftermath, the military brass have come to fear the "Dover effect": the ongoing stream of war dead arriving at Dover airbase...

—RABBI DANIEL A. WEINER
Seattle Post-Intelligencer, 2/4/2004

In Seattle, a photographer shoots coffins
coming off the conveyor belt, baggage
of the C130. Streaming stripes blur
in the fuel doused air, like the pin-striped coats
of a barber shop quartet in Iowa or Ohio.
One flap of the flag flies up from the makeshift
casket. A guard, startled, tucks it down.

That night I dream I'm a coffin counter,
but the coffins won't stop coming.
Down and down from the belly of the plane,
they flood the tarmac. The dead are unhappy.

Where are the cameras to light their return,
to parade their image across the globe?
Corpses fling open their coffins. Flags float
upward like air balloons, each maimed body –
all its parts following. Like a morbid Magritte,
the sky fills with an eye, a leg, a prosthetic arm.
Infantry, supply clerks, cooks, guards – they are home
they say. They are finally home. Where is their welcome?
I try to explain how it is now, but all I hear
are the airstreams that pierce their bones.

Audacity

for Peggy

Of course it was raining. She was frantic to get to Canada,
on an expired passport, her husband in a coma.
The nurses said there was no brain activity. It's a blur
to her, but I remember our scramble to the county clerk,
the drive into New York, her size zero frame so brittle
I thought with a sudden slam on the breaks
her spine could snap. Then the long wait
in a dingy building, a child screeching four lines over.
She had to get to him. We both knew they heard these stories
everyday. Yet she held a ticket as if we were on a deli line.
She'd slip out for a smoke, puff a few, then stamp it out
hoping the number hadn't been called.
Who would tell her not to smoke now.

That night, she called from the hospital.
She said he was gone, that she couldn't smell
him. Stunned by how quickly our loves can leave us,
she had them raise his body temperature,
donate his eyes, his heart, his liver, his lung.
I imagined her next to his bed, machines pumping away,
a 6'7" man reduced to parts, and I wondered
about the long months ahead,
my alone different from her alone.

How would she reseed the yard, haul in the wood?
How would she place herself in that house without him?

Yet even then, I knew she would date again.
To risk it all, to get the love prize,
is to pay dearly when its gone.
Those like me who play it safe
marvel at the enormous gamble it takes.

A Comfort

for Bill

I heard of a woman who after being left
for the fourth time, closed the door,
then tried to hang herself. Her brother
brought her a beagle from the pound.
He worried what he would do with the dog,
if she tried again. Or what if the dog died?

My friend has eight cats and now a dog.
There have been lovers, and the longing
for a partner to share coffee with a Sunday Times.
He tells about summer afternoons, when
the neighborhood boys played baseball.
He hated baseball, could never throw a good pitch.
Instead, his mother let him read her magazines.
He'd sit on their porch lost in articles like
"Can This Marriage Be Saved" that stringent
gender role always present, always an indictment
that might never leave his father's lips. Parched
by the heat of an Iowa summer, he sprawled
across the plastic flowered chase, skinny legs
marked by mosquito bites and scrapes.

How far we travel from those early years
depends – some say genetics; some say luck.
When my friend gets home from work,
he lights the wood stove. Cats pile around him,
nuzzle his arms as he strikes a match.

Grey Hair

It takes time to love
that image in the mirror—
grizzled strands, wild threads
in the dark tuft of my own life.
What strange beauty claims these years.

On the Barrier Beach at Dusk

for Pam

Distracted, I scan all fence posts
for that damn snowy owl,
stumble trying to keep pace with you.
You think I cannot hear,
over the whip and slap of waves.
What can I say against such worry?

If only we were children
bare feet padding over the dunes:
you, an empress, exotic in green silk.
could concoct a magic pulp
coconut oil and course grained sand.
With your thumb you'd trace
a gritty crown across my forehead.

Giddy, I would twirl for you
until that setting star fire merged
with the squeak and squeal of our delight.

Dawn Trembles

After her night vigil, she dresses quietly,
covers him except for his bare feet
which he hates to have restrained.
Like a boy, his socks slip out of the quilt.

She heads down to the boardwalk.
where the wind has blown the dunes
to ridges. She thinks of the arêtes
she saw in Montana, knife-like ridges,
remnants of a glacial freeze above the plains.
.

Yesterday cloud cover gave her refuge.
Warm air against cold tidal waves
fogged the town in for the night.
She nearly slept. But today
 she can feel her own tremors
as the sun ruptures the horizon.

How will she live without him?
How will she let him go?

The Long Married

for Joe V

He leans over the table, barely awake,
hearing her worry—the house, her brothers,
the estate. A cup of black coffee
propped in his hand, what can he say
with so much loss already upon her.
He knows nothing other than this love.
He would drive her to New Mexico or Florida, anything
to get her away from here. But she's grounded
by the dead and the living. No drive can cure that.

So he sits, one bare foot over his knee
toes flexed; haplessly, he listens.
Not even his wide love can quell her demons.
But there are days when she turns to him
so fierce, so resilient, and he knows even a wind
like the Williwaw cannot blow them apart.

Red Terrier Chasing Birds

for Crosby

Bounding at robins, sparrows,
he chases anything with wings.

Impervious to his inability to fly,
he ascends on hind legs
triangle ears lifting up.

Anguish

(for Adam W., wherever he might be)

He sat in the back row, blonde hair covering one eye.
Always late, he'd slip into his seat, hide behind his monitor.
Already, I was tuning him out until the paper about his mom.
I have to keep telling her she is still beautiful", he wrote.
Then he missed three classes in a row, didn't email
a revision. I thought he was gone for good.

One night, after the clocks had *fallen back,*
he came just as class ended. No book, hair disheveled,
his boss had made him work late. By then in the dark hall,
the gilded letters "President's Office" shone on the locked
glass doors behind him. He stood at an angle to me
staring downward, sneakers untied. Then like some mythic figure
his arms rose above him — *I didn't even stop to clean-up,* he said.

Still, no work from him.
The last class before I failed him,
he sat next to my computer.
Well, there's no-one else to blame, he shrugged.
His fingers still bore remnants of axle grease,
as if no solvent could ever wash it off.

Why I Love the New York Yankees

(for Jeannie LeBlanc — avid Red Socks fan)

Biloxi, Mississippi, 1959, the fan club letter came. The blue
inked scrawls of Roger Maris and Mickey Mantle elated me.
Mother was not thrilled. Why the *Yankees*? How could I explain
the joy coming from the transistor radio when we could never escape
the derision of that word. My mother's Boston *r's* marked her,
while I inadvertently slipped into a kind of slow drawl

my vowels stretching out as long as my legs.
There was so much wrong with me then.
I was Catholic. I asked too many questions.
My neighbor drove me to see the colored kids' new school
to prove that they wanted to be separate from us. They wanted
their own school, their own water fountains, to sit with their own
at the lunch counter or the back of the bus. The Yankees
stirred up trouble, I was told. They ought to go back North
or some of that trouble might spill over on them.

Mother urged me not to talk with little Negro boys
when we went out. *Honey, they could get beaten up or worse.*
I knew she meant the fire hoses we'd seen on our
black-and-white TV mowing down other kids my age. I didn't
know about Emmet Till then. I just knew how even the simplest
words could strike like flint, igniting
any dark-skinned person's world.

So when I opened that paper and saw pictures of the gleaming
team, cocky in pin stripes, I was part of Yankee magic.
The way the radio announcer shouted it, his gusto
was unlike the sting in the word I heard everywhere else —

a sales clerk in the five-and-dime as my mother picked up her
package, the whisper under the teacher's breath when she told
the principal about me, or Tommy Lee Mays at recess who chased me
with a dead water moccasin. *Yankee, Yankee*, he'd squeal,
drawing the word out over the playground.

Red Berries in Winter

for Kristi

What is this gangly tree outside my window?
Berries crystallize in the ice storm. Everything glistens.
More rust than red, through raucous wind, freezing rain,
they adhere to bare branches like beads of love.

Last night, a friend called near midnight, her son caught
in a snow squall on Lookout Pass. I remembered
the winter treks home, and a story of a VW Beetle
in blizzard winds sliding off the snow-slicked road.

I've been reading the ancients – how one tried to cheat
death. My friend calls again. Chains weighting the tires
her son tucked his car behind a snowplow,
edged his way in the spew of salt and sand.

I picture his hulking form over the steering wheel, then
that hesitation—before boot pushes pedal,
slush-pelted windshield eclipsing his vision.

Aftermath

for Jim Haba upon his retirement

How you scared me, your hand, fingers open, palm
widened, a pen nearby. That long table where
we all gathered with our slips of poems... How my life
fractured and filled with all you brought to it.

I'd like to believe we are like that hand—
always ready to hold fast. Maybe that's what the hand
can do, but the heart, there's always a cost to the heart in
the swell and flow of each chamber's pulsing.
Aorta, ventricle, each beat cycling, some capillaries
so thin they could burst.

In the years of wild beating, there's all that motion,
and then it slows.
        So what if we are stunned
in the slowing, in the long release? What if each loss
wears down an artery wall, hardens plaque
against vein—muscle starved in the thinning flow?
What else could we have done?

Whatever rhythm lingers, may it find its way
into your own poems; may it tweak and tune
those ineffable elements we call time or loss or love.

Winter

for Linda

Persephone wanted to return.
It seemed a simple thing:
take the pomegranate seed, swallow it
leave the underworld if only for a season.
So hungry was she, not just for sunlight,
but for her meadow where jonquil

sprayed the hillside. Hers is a story
for the young. Toes and fingers never numb—
they need no coats, no sweaters
in the evening's chill. Such freedom.

But we who are older live in layers—
cotton, wool, silk against skin.
See how the silhouette of bare oak
stems a December sky, brittle frame
yielding fully like every dying thing.

Acknowledgements

"Grading Papers at 10 p.m." and "Why I Love Birthday Cake".
Paterson Literary Review#40. Summer 2012.

Why I Love the New York Yankees". Honorable Mention: New
Jersey Poetry Prize Contest. Journal of NJ Poets. 2012

"And When I Die". Honorable Mention: Tiferet Poetry Contest
(Judge; Alicia Ostriker). Digital Issue. Nov. 2011

"Once My Husband". *U.S. 1 Worksheets*. Princeton, NJ 2009

"Sandy Hook Lighthouse" & "When the Body Takes Over".
Paulinskill Poetry Project. Spring, 2009.

"Forsaken" and "Payback". *Journal of New Jersey Poets*. Issue
46, 2009.

"Dawn Trembles". *Community College Moment*. Vol. 8, Spring
2008.

"Death Rites". *Journal of New Jersey Poets*. Nominated for a
Pushcart Prize, Sept. '07

"Membrane" and "The Mourner". *Tiferet*. Issue 4. Spring 2007

"On the Barrier Beach". *Spindrift*. Walt Whitman Poetry
Anthology, Fall 2006.

"Western Union". *Edison Literary Review*. Issue 5. Spring 2006.

"Kaleidoscope" (formerly "Telescope"). *The Fourth River*.

Chatham College. Woodland Road, Pittsburgh, PA. 15232. Spring '06.

"The Ether". *Rough Places Plain: Poems Of The Mountains*, edited by Margot Wizansky. Salt Marsh Press. 2006

"Losing the Horizon" *Mercy Of Tides: Poems For A Beach House*, edited by Margot Wizansky, illustrations by J.P. Powel. Salt Marsh Press, 2003.

"What We Regret". *Red River Review*, www.RedRiverReview.com, August, 02

"Late Bloomer". *Snowapple Journal,* Vermont, Spring 2002

❧

Thanks to the poets and friends who've sustained me in this work: *Us Four*, my poetry group; fellow poets from Geraldine R. Dodge, Warren Wilson, and Sussex County, for Pam and Harry Bernard. And a special thanks to Jan, my publisher, a very brave soul.

About the Author

PRISCILLA ORR, author of *Jugglers & Tides*, also from Hannacroix Creek Books, is a recipient of fellowships from New Jersey State Council on the Arts and Yaddo, a Dodge Poet, and twice nominated for a Pushcart Prize. Orr's poems have been awarded and have appeared in *Southern Poetry Review, Nimrod, Worcester Review, Tiferet,* and other journals. A full professor of English at Sussex County Community College (SCCC), Orr also publishes book reviews.

OTHER BOOKS BY PRISCILLA ORR PUBLISHED BY HANNACROIX CREEK BOOKS THAT YOU MIGHT ENJOY

Jugglers and Tides: Poems

"Priscilla Orr's poems are full of feelings, sympathy, and a keen sense of the impermanence of love and life."
—Reginald Gibbons, Frances Hooper Chair in the Arts and Humanities Professor of English, Classics, Spanish, & Portuguese at NORTHWESTERN UNIVERSITY

"Orr's poetry is unflinching in its direct gaze at the raw material of a woman's experience. Readers will recognize their own truths expressed in a new way."
—Donna Perry, Ph.D., *Backtalk: Women Writers Speak Out*